STOP THINKING LIKE RAINY MONDAY AND
START LIVING LIKE SUNNY FRIDAY!
FIND MORE FUNNY THOUGHTFUL STUFF AT
ALELOOP DOT COM

CREATED BY ALELOOP

WRITTEN BY DAMIAN ALIBERTI

CHARACTERS BY ALEJANDRA LEIBOVICH

ISBN: 978-1-7340188-0-6
LCCN: 2019914794

PRODUCED ON ALELOOP'S MIND.

WITH LOVE

DEDICATED TO MY CAT, THE BROTHER OF MY CAT,
MY DOG AND ALL THE MANY CREATURES
THAT INSPIRE ME INCLUDING
MY HUSBAND, SON, TEAM, FRIENDS AND FAMILY.

ALELOOP–

MEETING ALELOOP'S ADORABLE MISCHIEVOUS CHARACTERS
HAS BEEN BEEN A LIFE CHANGING EXPERIENCE IN EVERY
POSSIBLE WAY. NOT JUST BECAUSE THEY MAKE ME LAUGH AND
LEARN. ALSO, THEY ARE A REFLECTION OF ALL THE GOOD AND THE
WONDERFUL IN THE WORLD. AND THEY REPRESENT ALL THE GREAT
IDEAS INSIDE ALL OF US.

DAMIAN–

EVERY NEXT LEVEL
OF YOUR LIFE
WILL NEED A
DIFFERENT, BOLDER, STRONGER
VERSION OF YOU.*

(* NOT SEXIER, 'CAUSE THAT WILL BE SO UNFAIR
FOR THE REST OF THE WORLD)

LEADERSHIP IS LIKE SOCCER. . .
YOU NEED PERSEVERANCE
PASSION, STRATEGY, DEDICATION

AND BALLS

aleloop

THE FIRST PERSON YOU ARE LEADING

IS YOURSELF.

IF YOU BELIEVE, OTHERS WILL TOO.

ONE DAY YOU ARE YOUNG
AND BEAUTIFUL.

AND THEN SUDDENLY
YOU HAVE A FAVORITE GROCERY STORE.

IF YOU TALK ABOUT IT
IT'S AN IDEA.

IF YOU SEE IT
IT'S POSSIBLE.

IF YOU SCHEDULE IT
IT'S REALLY HAPPENING.

THINGS ARE NOT GOING AS EXPECTED

I DEMAND TO SPEAK
WITH LIFE'S MANAGER!

EVERY DAY IS A GIFT.

BUT TODAY I EXPECTED
TO GET A TRIP TO HAWAII,
NOT TO DO MID-YEAR REVIEWS.

OFFLINE IS THE NEW LUXURY

LIFE BEGINS

EXACTLY AT THE END
OF YOUR COMFORT ZONE

NOT EVERYONE
CAN BE FAMOUS.

BUT EVERYBODY CAN DO
GREAT THINGS.

IT ALWAYS SEEMS

IMPOSSIBLE

UNTIL

SOMEONE

~~DOES IT.~~

YOU DO IT

aleloop

YOU ARE STANDING STILL

OR EVEN WORSE

YOU ARE

STEPPING

BACKWARDS

WHAT DOES
AN ENTREPRENEUR
AND EVERYONE ELSE
HAVE IN COMMON?

NOTHING.

INNOVATION MEANS I HAVE TO CHANGE ?!?

BECOMING A LEADER
IS LIKE EATING
PEANUT BUTTER
WITH YOUR FINGERS

CHALLENGING BUT DELICIOUS.

TO BE SEEN

VISION NEEDS TO BE FOLLOWED

BY ACTION

THERE ARE 3 WAYS

TO INFLUENCE HUMAN BEHAVIOR:

1. WITH INSPIRATION
2. WITH EXAMPLE
3. WITH MUFFINS

DO SOMETHING

TODAY

YOUR

FUTURE-SELF

WILL THANK YOU FOR

IF YOU WANT
TO CHANGE
SOMETHING
CHANGE YOURSELF

BE THE KIND OF PERSON

YOU

WOULD LIKE

TO FOLLOW

DON'T BE BUSY.
BE PRODUCTIVE.

WE ARE KEPT FROM REACHING OUR GOALS

NOT BY OBSTACLES

BUT BY OUR OWN

SELF-LIMITING BELIEFS.

aleloop

DON'T LET OTHER PEOPLE

DEFINE WHAT YOU CAN BECOME OR ACCOMPLISH

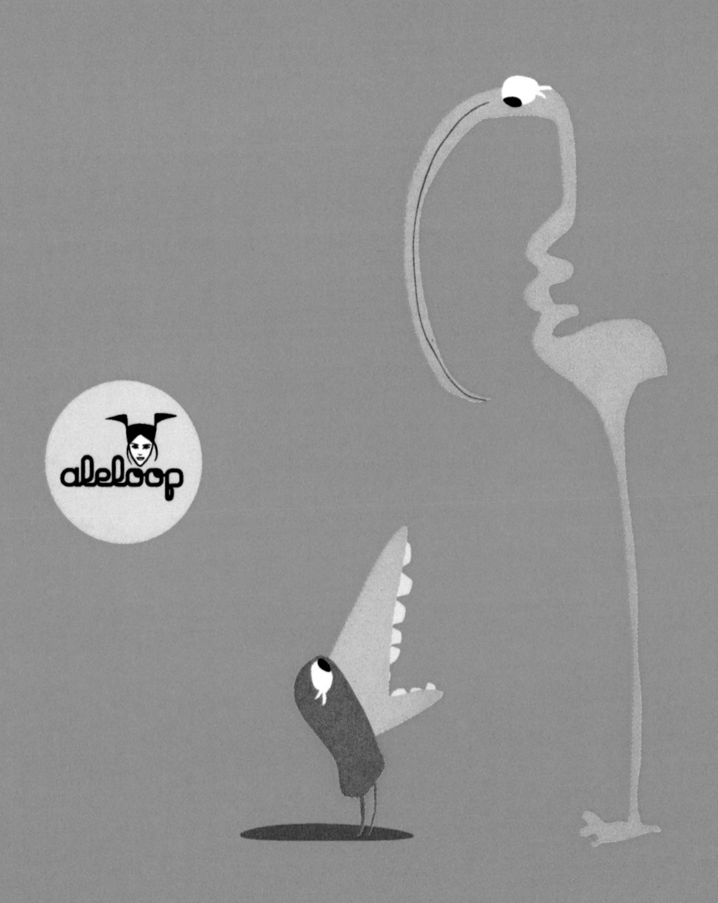

DIFFICULTIES PROVOKE LEADERSHIP.

USE THEM WISELY

SOMETIMES I FEEL LIKE

DROPBOX

IS NOT MY FRIEND

AVOID THINGS

THAT MAKE YOU LOOK FAT

LIKE MIRRORS

(AND SCALES...)

(BUT DON'T FORGET TO LOOK AT YOUR NUMBERS!)

THE SMALLEST

STEP

CAN TAKE YOU IN THE

RIGHT

DIRECTION

SOMETIMES YOU MIGHT FEEL
LIKE NO ONE IS THERE FOR YOU.

BUT IT'S NOT TRUE

EMAIL

IS ALWAYS THERE WAITING FOR YOU.

DISCIPLINE IS REMEMBERING WHAT YOU WANT

SMILE

IF YOU WANT TO BE HAPPY

BE HAPPY.

THE ONLY WAY
TO NOT WORRY
ABOUT BEING SUCCESSFUL...

IS TO BE SIGNIFICANT.

SOMETIMES

THE BEST YOU CAN DO IS

RELAX

AND HAVE A SLICE OF CAKE.

I'M NOT CRAZY.

I ONLY TALK TO MYSELF

WHEN I NEED EXPERT ADVICE

TO DO LIST

1. DRINK COFFEE
2. INSPIRE MY TEAM
3. WEAR PANTS

I'M NOT SHORT.

I JUST WRITE SHORT EMAILS.

YOU HAVE TO

BELIEVE IT

BEFORE

YOU CAN SEE IT.

NEVER TRUST AN ATOM

THEY MAKE UP

EVERYTHING

IT'S ALL

FUN AND GAMES

UNTIL WE RUN OUT OF

COFFEE

WHEN YOUR ACTIONS
INSPIRE OTHERS TO...
LEARN MORE,
DO MORE AND
BECOME MORE.

YOU ARE A LEADER.

The perfect antidote to boring posters about leadership

MONEY WON'T BUY

HAPPINESS

BUT IT CAN AFFORD ME AN

EXECUTIVE ASSISTANT

THE WORLD IS FULL OF

MAGICAL THINGS

LIKE

ROLLER SKATES

AND SOMEONE IN YOUR STAFF
REALLY GOOD WITH EXCEL

EVERYDAY BEGINS WITH AN ACT OF

COURAGE AND HOPE

IT'S CALLED

GETTING OUT OF BED.

REPEATING SMALL

HABITS

CAN CREATE SOMETHING.

LIKE A BELLY

YOUR IMAGINATION

TRAILER

OF YOUR LIFE

aleloop

THERE IS NO LEADERSHIP WITHOUT FAILURE

THE ONLY WAY
TO GET THINGS STARTED
IS TO QUIT BLAH BLAH
AND BEGIN TO MOVE
YOUR...

I WAS GOING TO

TAKE OVER

THE WORLD

THIS MORNING

BUT I OVERSLEPT.

DON'T BE SO HARD ON YOURSELF

REMEMBER

THE MOM IN E.T. HAD A FRIGGIN' ALIEN LIVING IN HER HOUSE FOR A WEEK.

AND SHE DIDN'T NOTICE.

ABOUT DAMIAN ALIBERTI

DAMIAN IS A BIG KID WITH A SMALL BEARD,
A NATURAL STORYTELLER, ARTIST AND AN AVID COMIC BOOK READER WITH A HEART FOR BAKING COOKIES, MOVIES, AND WRITING. HE BRINGS HIS LOVE FOR STORYTELLING, AND PASSION FOR LIFE TO THE WORLD OF ALELOOP.

BORN AND RAISED IN BUENOS AIRES, HE LIVED ABROAD MANY YEARS WORKING IN ADVERTISING AS A COPYWRITER AND DESIGNER, VIDEO GAMES AND CREATIVE MEDIA. HE'S AN AWARD-WINNING DESIGNER, VIDEO GAME ENTREPRENEUR, AND CHOCOLATE ENTHUSIAST.

HE EMIGRATED TO THE USA AND TEAMED WITH CARTOON NETWORK LATIN AMERICA F OR MORE THAN A DECADE (ALMOST BECOMING A CARTOON HIMSELF) AS A WRITER AND ARTIST. LATER OPENED HIS OWN STUDIO CREATING VIDEO GAMES FOR NICKELODEON, STARBUCKS, AND LEGO AND EVEN APPEARED AS A GUEST IN MASTERCHEF MAKING TRADITIONAL ARGENTINIAN FOOD TV SHOW.

LATELY, HE'S BEEN FOCUSING ON EDUCATION AND MENTORING FOR KIDS AND ADULTS, CREATING HIS OWN TOOLS AND BOARD GAMES. WORKING WITH ALELOOP AND HER ADORABLE MINIATURE MISCHIEF-MAKERS HAS BECOME MORE THAN A PASSION BUT A TRUE CALLING.
FROM MAKING PASTRIES TO ADULTHOOD ISSUES, HIS DISTINCTIVE HUMOR AND VOICE TRANSFORM EVERY-DAY SITUATIONS INTO A UNIQUE WORLD BEYOND AGE, LANGUAGE, AND CULTURE.

ABOUT

AWARD WINNING ANIMATOR, ENTREPRENEUR, AUTHOR, CARTOONIST, APPS-GAMES-SOFTWARE DEVELOPER AND SANDWICH LOVER, ALEJANDRA LEIBOVICH AKA ALELOOP, USES HER CREATIVITY OVER A WIDE RANGE OF FIELDS AND DISCIPLINES BECAUSE WHY DO JUST ONE THING WHEN THERE ARE SO MANY FREAKING COOL THINGS TO DO!

ALELOOP DIVIDES HER TIME BETWEEN WORKING ON A SCI-FI GRAPHIC NOVEL, PAINTING, DEVELOPING SOFTWARE AND TAKING ON SELECT ANIMATION AND DESIGN PROJECTS FOR CLIENTS INCLUDING MTV, NICKELODEN, CN, 7UP, DR. PEPPER, WOLVERINE, X-MEN, IRONMAN, NICKTOONS, ETC.

ALELOOP'S PRESS INCLUDES THE USA TODAY, CBS, DISCOVERY NEWS, MIAMI HERALD, MIAMI NEW TIMES, FOX DECO DRIVE, TREND HUNTER, SUNPOST, SUN SENTINEL, MOTOR TREND, AMONG MANY OTHERS.

ORIGINALLY FROM ARGENTINA, ALELOOP DECIDED TO KEEP HER THICK ENGLISH ACCENT AND HAS BEEN LIVING IN THE USA FOR THE BETTER HALF HER LIFE.
YOU CAN CATCH HER ALWAYS UP TO SOMETHING
AT ALELOOP.COM

Made in the USA
Monee, IL
08 December 2020